MERCURY
PLANETS IN OUR SOLAR SYSTEM
CHILDREN'S ASTRONOMY EDITION

SPEEDY
PUBLISHING

Speedy Publishing LLC
40 E. Main St. #1156
Newark, DE 19711
www.speedypublishing.com

Copyright 2015

Mercury is the closest planet to the Sun.

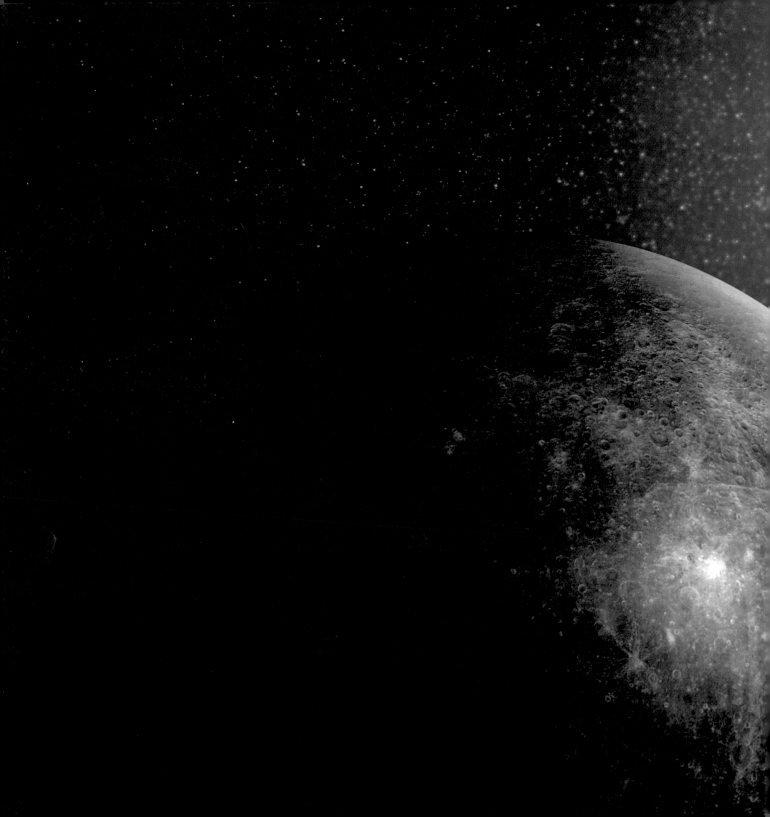

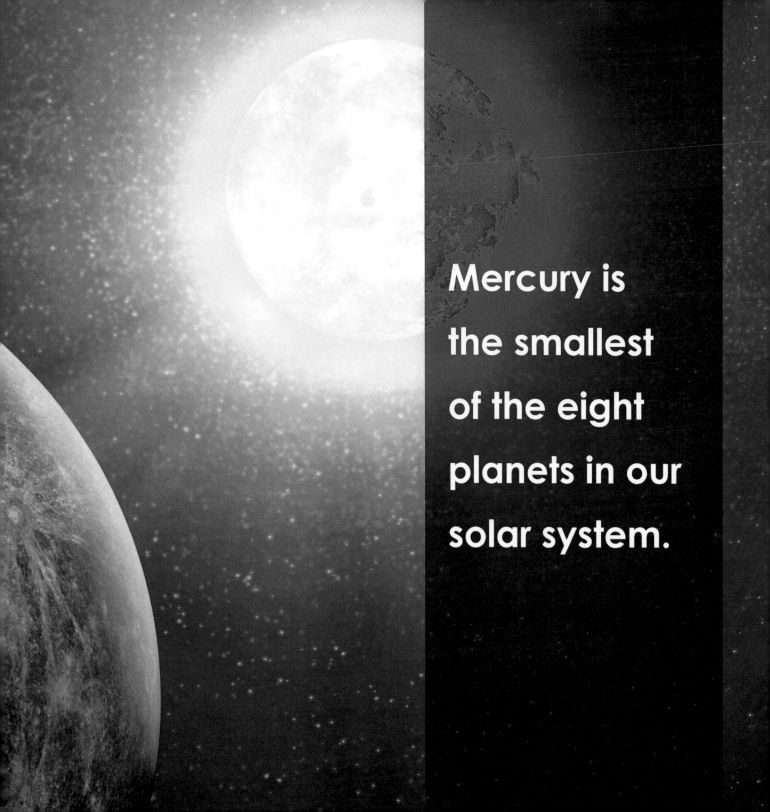

Mercury is
the smallest
of the eight
planets in our
solar system.

Mercury orbits around the Sun. Its orbit lasts for only 88 days.

The daytime temperature on Mercury is reaching over 400 Degrees Celsius.

At night, the temperatures plummet, dropping to -180 Degrees Celsius.

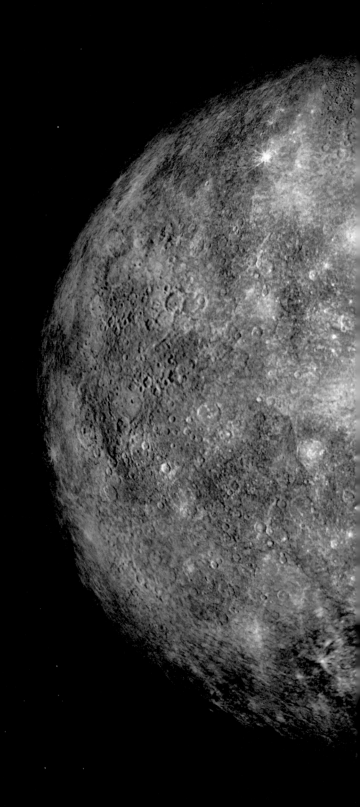

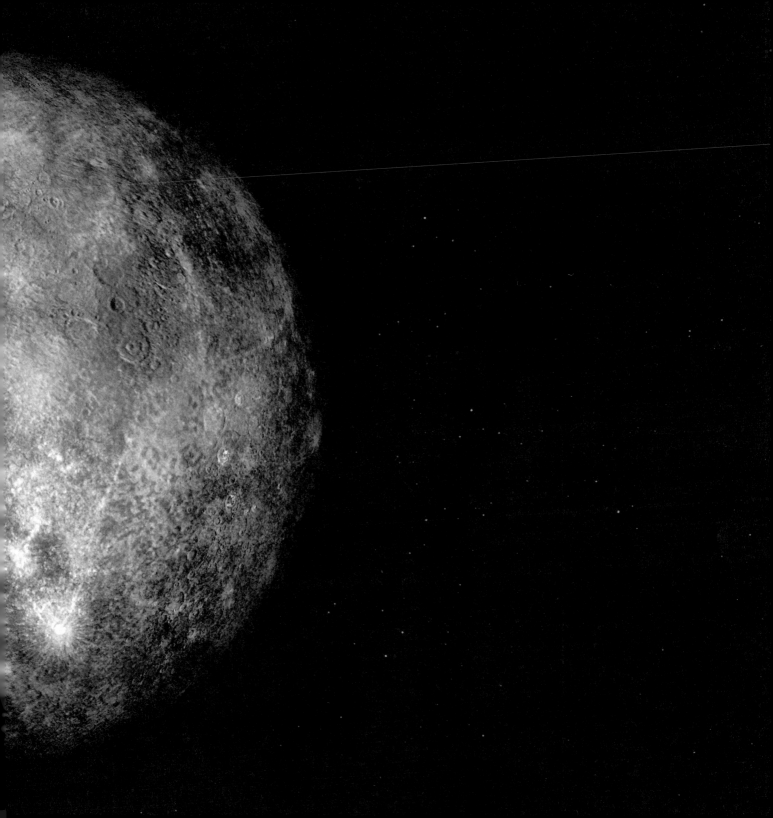

Mercury has no atmosphere which means there is no wind or weather to speak of.

When Mercury orbits the Sun, it travels 36 million miles in the 88 days of the orbit.

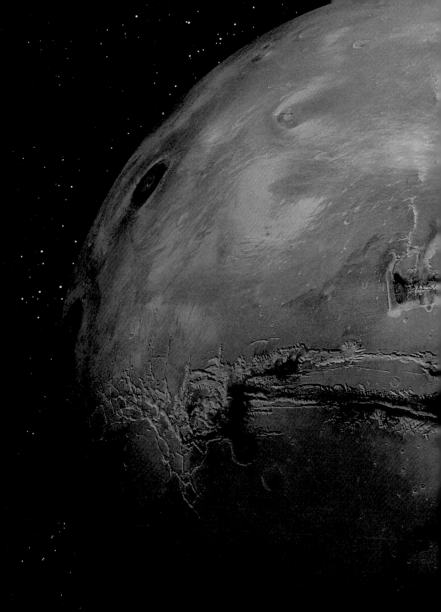

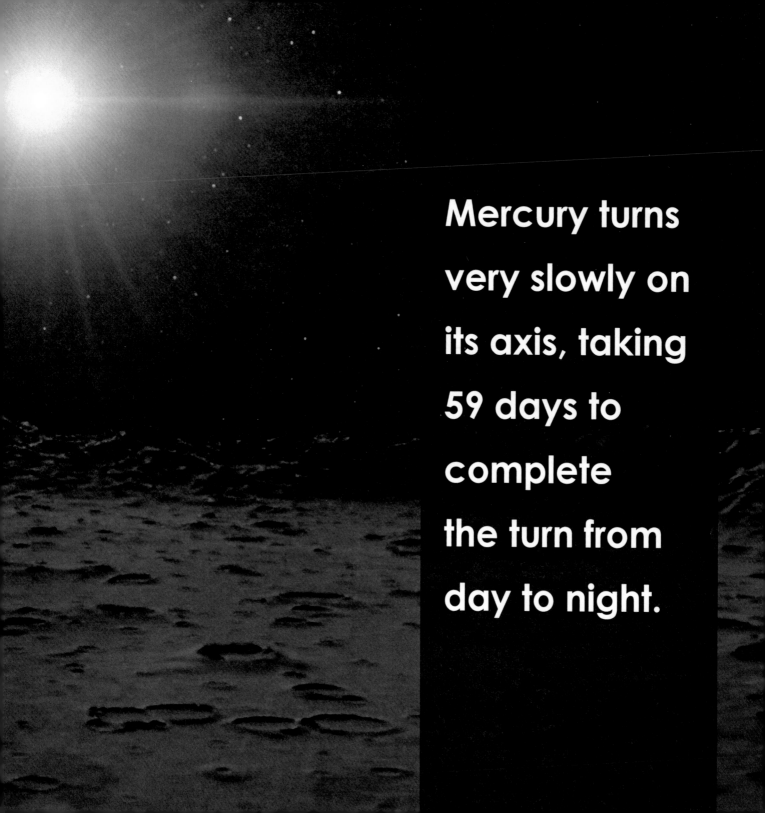

Mercury turns very slowly on its axis, taking 59 days to complete the turn from day to night.

Mercury has
no known
natural
satellites.

The planet is named after the Roman deity Mercury, the messenger to the gods.

Mercury
can appear
in Earth's
sky in the
morning or
the evening.

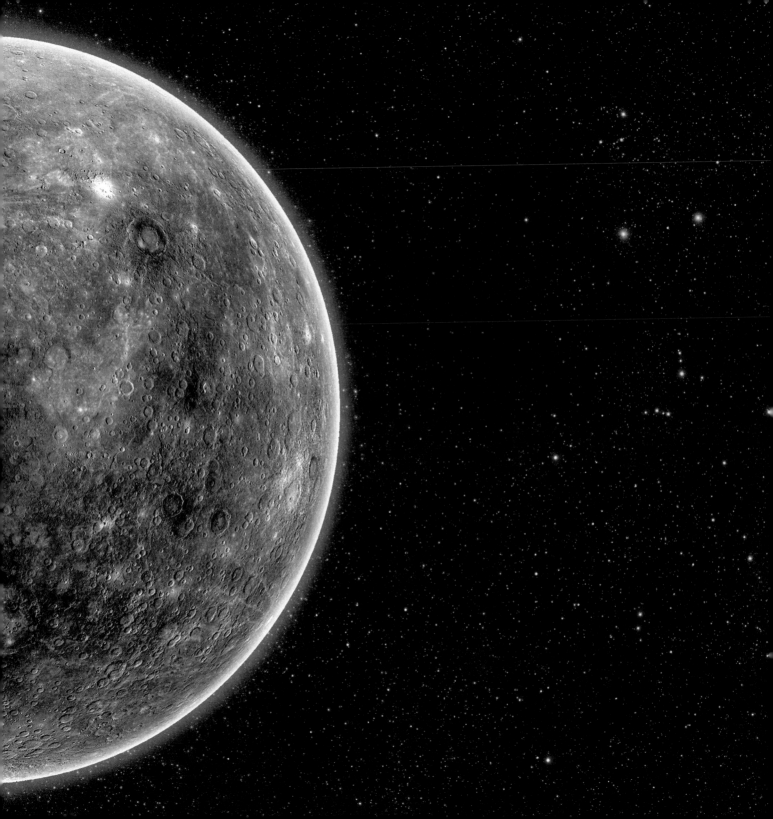

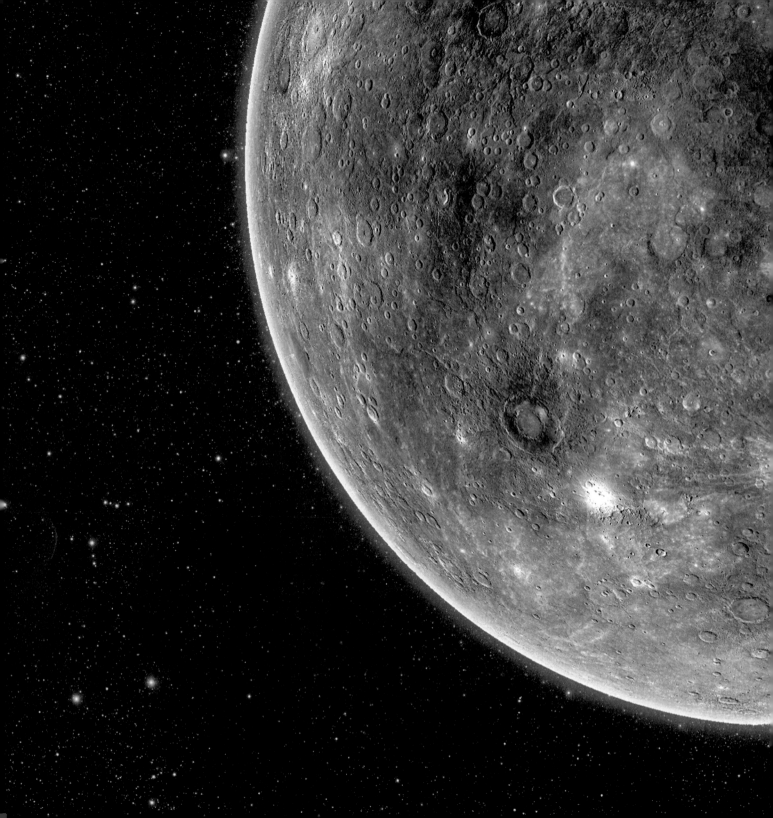

Mercury's core has a higher iron content than that of any other major planet in the Solar System.

Mercury was heavily bombarded by comets and asteroids during and shortly following its formation 4.6 billion years ago.

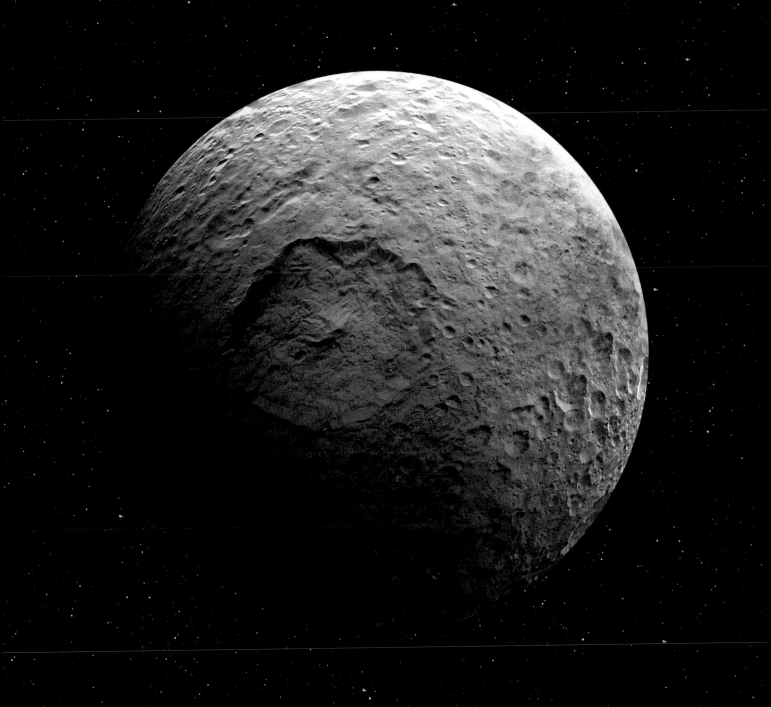

There is no water on the surface of Mercury.

There is also
no air on the
surface of
Mercury.

The first
photographs
of the surface
of Mercury
were taken
by NASA.

NASA's latest mission to Mercury is called Messenger. The Messenger entered Mercury's orbit in March 2011.

Mercury is one of five planets that can be seen without using a telescope.

Mercury
is only the
second
hottest
planet. Venus
experiences
higher
temperatures.